Courage:
A Redemption Story

To fiell
Washington is calling
you. You are such an
inspiration to many.
I see your voice resounding
to the masses. your words
will go deep into the hearts
of many. love you

Lacricia Darling

By Lacricia Darling

Publisher:
Self-Published by Lacricia Darling
ISBN: 979-8-9912736-0-2
Printed in the United States of America

Photography: Gabriel Sucre
Cover Design: "MA Rehman"
Book Formatting: "Samia Asif"
Editing: "Tall Pine Books"

First Edition

Disclaimer:
In sharing my story, I made the choice not to include certain names and details to protect the privacy of those involved. My intent is not to point fingers or dwell on past hurts, but to offer a message of hope and healing to anyone who needs it.
The experiences and reflections shared are my own, and any resemblance to actual persons, living or deceased, or actual events is purely coincidental unless expressly stated. This book is meant to inspire, encourage, and promote personal growth.

Scripture Quotations:
Scripture quotations are taken from various versions of the Bible, including New International Version (NIV), King James Version (KJV), English Standard Version (ESV). All rights reserved by the respective copyright holders.

DEDICATION

Yvette Pawnell

To my beloved niece, Yvette Pawnell,

Her courage in the face of stomach cancer inspired all who knew her.
You left us on February 28, 2024, but your spirit and strength continue
to light our paths. This book is dedicated to your memory—may it
inspire courage in others as you have in us.

CONTENTS

FOREWORD THERESA DEDMON

I am so glad you picked up this book. I believe it will guide you on your journey, both now and in the future. It's a journey filled with hope and promise.

To embark on this path, you must be willing to face your pain, trauma, and unmet needs. It's in the place of vulnerability that we encounter the comfort of Father God.

In life, we don't choose our parents or how they raised us, but we do get to choose how we "see" our lives—from the standpoint of redemption rather than brokenness. We have the power to decide what we do with our past: the good, the bad, and the ugly.

In her book, Courage: A Redemption Story, Lacricia reveals a truth many of us overlook because it's easier to avoid what has hurt us. But I believe pain has a purpose. The way to understand our hearts is to examine the fragmented parts of our journey and allow God to release His healing. This is what you will find in this book: a way to share your story and let God transform you into His likeness.

Many of us have learned to cope with trauma and pain by "sucking it up" or "faithing it," denying the pain we've endured. But this is not the way of the true Father. Remember the story of the prodigal son? The Father was waiting for his son to come home—not after he cleaned up his act, but while he was still penniless, having squandered his inheritance, which had been freely given by the Father.

Redemption is not needed when we have it all together or have proven ourselves. Redemption is needed when we are at our lowest, when others have hurt us deeply. This is why forgiveness will always be a part of our redemptive story.

In my own journey of brokenness, I grew up with a father who was verbally and physically abusive. When I came to Jesus and was filled with the Spirit, I understood God's heart to make me a new person, but I had no idea He wanted to heal the wounds of my past.

As I began to explore who Father God really was, I started experiencing all the wonderful blessings that can only come from a Good, Good Father. This revelation has led me to raise up many other creative dreamers, like Lacricia, who are eager to share their stories through art, poetry, music, dance, and writing as a way of "coming home."

One of the beautiful ways the Kingdom of God works is that whatever victory and supernatural empowerment I've received, I can pass on to others.

Scripture tells us to comfort others with the comfort we've been given.

So, let Lacricia's story guide you toward grace and rest in the Father's embrace. Let her breakthrough become your breakthrough!

It's time for courage to rise in your heart as God invites you to face every fear and lie that stands in your path. Allow His redemptive nature to heal your wounds until all you see is His face!

I am excited for you to lose yourself in these pages and find yourself in the process.

Theresa Dedmon
Author, Artist, Speaker
Theresa@theresadedmon.com

INTRODUCTION

Welcome to a journey of heartache, hardship, and healing. "Courage: A Redemption Story" is not just a tale of overcoming the odds; it is a testament to the unyielding strength of the human spirit when guided by God's grace. In these pages, you will discover not only my story, but also a mirror reflecting elements of your own struggles and triumphs.

This book begins in the shadows of absence—the void left by a father I never knew. From the early days of feeling unseen and misunderstood, my path seemed fraught with missteps and misunderstandings, leading me into relationships and situations where my light dimmed further under the weight of betrayal and abuse. But the narrative of my life took a dramatic turn, a testament to what can unfold when one is willing to confront their deepest pains under the gaze of a higher power.

Here, I share how the darkest moments of my life were intricately woven into a larger tapestry of redemption that I could only appreciate in hindsight. Through intimate encounters with God, who proved Himself as the Father to the fatherless, and through the transformative power of forgiveness and inner healing, I found a new way to walk—courageously.

This book is structured to take you through the various stages of my spiritual and emotional evolution:

- From confronting the deep-seated "Father's Gap" that marked my early years,
- Through the miraculous ways in which my faith was fortified and my burdens lifted,
- To the blossoming of a life marked by courage, new beginnings, and a profound sense of belonging,
- And finally, to a place of continuous gratitude and praise, standing firm in the role of a spiritual beacon for others who might still be wandering in the dark.

Each chapter is an invitation to explore not just the events that shaped me, but also the lessons that can liberate you. Whether you are struggling with your own gaps, filled with pain, walking through the process of healing, or seeking to deepen your connection with God...this story is for you.

"Courage: A Redemption Story" is more than my memoir—it is a call to anyone who hears it to rise, redeem, and to transform, through the indomitable power of faith. The word "indomitable" means impossible to subdue or defeat. It describes someone or something that cannot be overcome, showing great courage, strength, and resilience in the face of challenges or difficulties which I have shown and you can too.

As you turn these pages, may you find the courage to face your own story with a renewed spirit and an open heart.

Do You Need God's Redemption in Your Life?

Have you ever felt lost, rejected, burdened by your past mistakes, or in need of a new beginning? Do you find yourself longing for forgiveness, healing, acceptance and a new sense of purpose? If so, you are not alone. Many of us reach a point in our lives where we desperately need redemption—a profound transformation that only God can provide.

UNDERSTANDING REDEMPTION

Redemption is a profound concept in Christianity that signifies being saved from sin, error, or evil. It's about being delivered from the bondage of sin through the sacrifice of Jesus Christ. His death on the Cross and resurrection provide the means for our redemption, offering us forgiveness and a new life.

My Personal Journey of Redemption: My story is one of deep personal transformation. I remember a time when I felt completely lost, rejected, and burdened by the weight of my sins and past mistakes. It was during one of my lowest moments that I encountered God's redeeming love. Through prayer, repentance, and seeking His presence, I experienced a profound sense of forgiveness, acceptance and renewal. God's grace and love washed over me, and I felt a new sense of purpose and identity in Him.

Biblical Stories of Redemption: The Bible is full of stories of redemption. One of my favorites is the story of the Prodigal Son (Luke 15:11-32). This parable beautifully illustrates God's unconditional love and forgiveness. No matter how far we stray, God is always ready to welcome us back with open arms. Similarly, the story of Ruth and Naomi shows how God can redeem even the most difficult circumstances, turning loss and despair into hope and restoration.

Theological Insights: Redemption is the act of redeeming or atoning for a fault or mistake. It involves paying the price to set someone free, saving them from sin, error, or evil. Redemption also means regaining possession of something in exchange for payment or clearing a debt. God paid the price for our sins and offers us redemption. We all have areas in our lives that need God's redemption, making our relationship with Christ unique.

Redemption occurs when God restores something lost or stolen in our lives. Redemption is a central theme throughout the Bible. From the Old Testament to the New Testament, God's plan for humanity's redemption unfolds. In the Old Testament, we see God's covenant with Israel, promising redemption and restoration. The New Testament reveals the fulfillment of that promise through Jesus Christ, who redeems us through His sacrificial death and resurrection.

Application: Experiencing redemption is not just a one-time event but a continuous journey. It involves daily surrender, prayer, and seeking a deeper relationship with Jesus. Repentance is a crucial step in this journey, acknowledging our sins and turning away from them. As we grow in our faith, we experience the transformative power of God's redemption in every aspect of our lives.

Impact on Relationships: Redemption not only changes us individually, but also transforms our relationships. In my marriage, experiencing God's redeeming love helped heal wounds and restore trust. It taught me the importance of forgiveness, grace, and love, in building a healthy relationship. Redemption brings healing and reconciliation, impacting our families and communities.

EMBRACING COURAGE

Telling my story required immense courage. There were times when I felt vulnerable and afraid, unsure of how others would perceive me. But I knew that my story of redemption could inspire and encourage others.

Prophetic Words and Confirmation: I received several prophetic words about how God wanted me to share my story. Initially, I thought this was absurd. I didn't see myself as an author. I kept putting it off until I received a word from Luba from Bethel Church in Redding, CA. She said, "God said it's time. No more waiting; you need to share your story." A fear came upon me, and I knew this wasn't about me—it was about those who needed to hear my story. So, I began my journey, and here is my story.

Defining Courage: Courage is not the absence of fear but the strength to face it. The Bible encourages us to be strong and courageous, as in Joshua 1:9: "Have I not commanded you? Be strong and courageous. Do not be afraid; do not be discouraged, for the Lord your God will be with you wherever you go." Courage is about trusting in God's presence and power, even in the midst of fear.

The Role of Faith in Courage: My faith in God gave me the courage to share my story. There were moments when I felt overwhelmed by fear and doubt, but I leaned on God's strength. Prayer and scripture provided comfort and reassurance, reminding me that God was with me. Knowing that my story could bring hope and healing to others motivated me to step out in faith.

Encouraging Others: I want to encourage you to be courageous in your own journey. Whatever challenges you face, know that God is with you. He can turn your pain into purpose and your struggles into testimonies of His grace. Don't be afraid to share your story. Your experiences can inspire and uplift others, bringing glory to God.

Impact: Since sharing my story, I've heard from many others who found courage and hope through my journey. Their testimonies remind me of the power of vulnerability and authenticity. When we share our stories, we create a ripple effect of encouragement and transformation, impacting lives in ways we may never fully realize.

Ephesians 1:7 (NIV):
"In him we have redemption through his blood,
the forgiveness of sins,
in accordance with the riches of God's grace."

Yellow Skies

REDEMPTION POEM

Redemption is like yellow skies in my eyes,

God's prism, no more schisms.

He came and removed every bitter root

in my cortex while I was in my vortex.

I thought it'd be a fight to see His beauty in my sight.

Seeing His Glory in my worry,

doubting His victory in my life,

but as my confidence grew,

The beauty that I knew transformed into His form,

dispelling false alarms.

His joy flowed in me like a river beyond my control.

I was never told I could be bold as a lion.

Uncovered in my sheath lie mysteries beneath it all.

No longer will I fall; I have risen above,

Free to be who He created me to be.

Part 1:

The Father's Gap - Understanding My Past

Chapter 1

THE MISSING FATHER

Psalms 147:3
He heals the brokenhearted and binds up their wounds.

GROWING UP IN EAST ST. LOUIS

I remember playing outside with my nephews, niece, and neighborhood friends until the streetlights came on. Once that light flickered on, it signaled that I had to leave my friends still playing in the streets. Our two-story red brick house next to a playground stands out the most in my memories. The house, with its creaky floors and cozy kitchen, was a haven of warmth and love.

We had a home-cooked meal nearly every day, and the aroma of my mother's cooking filled the air. During holidays, we gathered in the living room, playing cards until the wee hours of the morning, with me often emerging as the winner in the game of Spades. Despite the challenges outside, our home was filled with peace and security. In our small living area, I found solace and strength.

UNDERSTANDING MY PAST

Growing up in East St. Louis, IL, I didn't have a biological father in my home. My stepfather lived with us, but I didn't have a father-daughter relationship with either of them. This absence left a void in me, leading to broken relationships with men and making me susceptible to mental and physical abuse. I didn't understand how a woman should be treated.

This pattern continued for years until I gave my life to Christ. I yearned for the joy of sitting on my Father's lap, to feel His heartbeat as I lay on His chest. Messages about the Father's love were often preached, but I couldn't comprehend how to receive it without ever having had a father in my life. This message became a broken record in my ears, and I grew frustrated whenever I heard it from the pulpit. Outwardly, I pretended to understand, but inside I still felt the deep loneliness of fatherlessness.

Then, during a prayer session, something extraordinary happened. I heard the Father speak to me, saying He would impart His love inside me. As I fell to the floor, I felt the warmth of His presence on my stomach. In that sacred moment, He said, "I am your Father. I love you even though your biological father has not been in your life. I have been with you from the beginning, and I am not like your earthly father."

This encounter marked the beginning of a transformative journey. Developing a father-daughter relationship with God started to heal the fatherlessness areas in my life. He assured me that I am fearfully and wonderfully made and that I am more than enough. "You are my daughter, and I love you," He said.

I often think of the story of Hagar and Ishmael in Genesis 16. Hagar slept with Abram to conceive a child for Sarai because she couldn't have children of her own. Knowing this, Hagar became prideful, which angered Sarai and caused her to send Hagar and Ishmael away. I thought of Hagar feeling rejected and unwanted, just as I felt without my father in my life. But even in those difficult moments, God sent an angel of the Lord to Hagar to minister to her, just as He did to me, even when I didn't know it. Jesus cares for us so much, and He wants us to feel His love and acceptance.

Growing up as a young girl, I dreamed of being married, having kids, and living the American dream as a defense lawyer. However, my dreams felt shattered growing up without a father in my life. My stepfather was present, but uninvolved. I lacked direction and guidance from a male father figure. My journey in school began as a shy, carefree little girl, but as I grew older, I became more aware of my circumstances and the absence of a father figure in my life.

We did many things together as a family—trips, fairs, theme parks, fishing—presenting ourselves as normal. However, beneath the surface, we were broken, and I thought this was normal. During seventh grade, I met a guy and we dated—it was fine. I met another guy and dated him too—it was fine. But it wasn't until I met the father of my kids that I realized the imperfections in relationships.

I met men who would mentally and physically abuse me, but I didn't know what to look for in a partner. Growing up my mom wasn't married and was already separated by the time I was born, so I didn't have a father figure early on. However, later in my life, my mom had a relationship with a man who became my stepfather. This experience gave me some insight into family dynamics, but it wasn't a constant representation, and I still struggled to understand what a healthy relationship looked like.

This lack of understanding caused me to form my own view of what a family unit was supposed to look like, which wasn't the way God intended. I endured years of abuse until I finally left those relationships. I mistakenly believed that getting abused was normal, or that it was somehow my fault. After each fight, I was told it would never happen again and that he would seek help, but he never did.

Consequently, I developed a fear of men, which affected my relationships with friends, family, and church leaders. I believed that if I kept my mouth shut, things would change, but they never did. It wasn't until I grew older and realized that I needed to change myself and remove certain people from my life that things began to improve. I had to reassess my view of people and understand what was acceptable and what wasn't in relationships.

Despite these challenges, I found solace and hope in God's word. Just as He sent an angel to Hagar, He sent mentors into my life who prayed for me and supported me. Through prayer and faith, I began to heal. My journey wasn't easy, but it was through these hardships that I discovered the true meaning of redemption.

Redemption occurs when God restores something lost or stolen in our lives. Personally, I have experienced God's redemption in my marriage, my health, and my family. Despite facing many challenges, God has shown me the true meaning of redemption. He delivers and redeems His people when they cry out to Him, especially after enduring lies, betrayal, deception, and other adversities from the enemy. Through my hardships, God has revealed what true redemption is.

I want to encourage anyone reading this who might be facing similar struggles. God's love and redemption are available to you, just as they were to me. No matter how deep the hurt or how long the journey, God is always there, ready to restore and heal.

Chapter 2

PATTERNS OF PAIN

THE MISSING FATHER

I remember one Christmas when my biological dad brought toys to my sister's house next door. I was happy to receive them, but I wondered why he was dropping off toys without coming to see me and my brother. My mom would always say, "He can't just show up; he need to call." Before my healing journey, I thought, "Who would say that? Who would deny me access to my dad?" I began to blame her for keeping him away. However, I later realized that even after her death, he remained absent from my life.

REALIZING HIS LOVE

Through inner healing, I realized he had a duty to abide by my mom's rules if he really wanted to see us. I thought he never loved me until I had an encounter where I saw him pushing me on a swing. I heard the Father say, "He did love you," not realizing that during that time, he had already passed away. I wondered why God was bringing all of this up now. I thought I was good; I didn't need a father. But once the journey started, I realized I always wanted him to be in my life. I longed for it, as did my younger brother, Chris.

SHUTTING DOWN

Looking back, I remember a time when my biological dad took me, my brother and niece to Six flags. We had a great time, filled with laughter and excitement. As we were leaving, he had a conversation with my brother that seemed significant, but I was too young to fully understand. I interjected, and my dad told me to shut up. After arriving home, I went into the house and never spoke to my dad again. Recently, I asked my brother about this incident. He said I was mad and that I didn't want to talk to our dad again. I had forgotten about this, and learning about it made me realize how it caused me to shut down and not use my voice the way God intended. I thought that if I talked or voiced my opinion, I would be told to shut up. It's daunting to realize how, when we are young, we can form beliefs that are not true about our Heavenly Father. It took me years to learn the truth.

WAITING ON THE PORCH

We moved to Texas, and I thought he never reached out to find us. One day, during a visit to East St. Louis, my sister and my mom saw him. He said he would come by to see me. I waited on the porch, and when he pulled up, I never left the porch. He never got out of his car, and then he just drove off. I wondered, why didn't he get out? In hindsight, I don't know what he was thinking, and I don't know why I never left the porch. Through a separate conversation, I learned that I can't go back in time to change this. I have to move forward, knowing that he did love me. During this time I discussed my feelings and experiences with Grant Stailey a respected elder at Bridgeway Church. Our conversations helped me find peace and understand the complexities of my relationship with my biological dad.

EARLY RELATIONSHIPS AND PREGNANCY

During my high school years, I began dating the father of my two oldest children. We would hang out occasionally, and our relationship seemed casual and carefree. However, one day I learned I was pregnant. The news filled me with fear and anxiety. I confided in my mom, and the family discussions that followed included whether I wanted to keep the baby or consider abortion. Growing up, conversations about abortions were not uncommon. After much contemplation, I decided to keep the baby.

A TUMULTUOUS RELATIONSHIP

My journey through pregnancy began with doctor visits and taking prenatal vitamins. Despite the significant milestone, my child's father never accompanied me to any of the appointments. My mom was my steadfast companion throughout this time. She even bought both a girl and a boy outfit since I chose not to know the baby's gender in advance. On September 15, 1990, my daughter Portia was born. The joy and excitement I felt seeing my precious little girl for the first time were indescribable. I stayed in the hospital for a few days before returning home. My child's father, who had left months earlier to live with his girlfriend in Missouri, was nowhere in sight. The girlfriend's mother called me, revealing multiple calls to my number on her phone bill and sharing that he had a newborn with her as well.

Eventually, he returned and expressed a desire to be involved in Portia's life, even though he initially denied she looked anything like him. As she grew older, her resemblance to him became undeniable. We moved in together, but the relationship turned tumultuous. He became increasingly aggressive, following me, and demanding I get out of the car angrily. The situation escalated one night when he dragged and hit me in front of our friends.

Repeated Patterns

I later discovered he was on drugs, and the abuse became more frequent and violent. He would steal my car, disappear for days, and began taking things from me. During this time, I became pregnant again, and the same destructive pattern continued. However, I reached my breaking point and decided I was done. He was living with another woman and had gotten her pregnant as well. Our relationship had turned into a scary rollercoaster ride, filled with hardships that cannot all be recounted here.

I ended the relationship, but he continued to find me, showing up and trying to force me to leave with him. This relationship was filled with many painful experiences, but through it all, I learned that God's hand was on me. After moving to San Antonio, I thought I was finally free, until I met the father of my third child. This journey of pain, resilience, and eventual redemption is a testament to the strength and courage I found within myself and through my faith.

MOVING TO SAN ANTONIO

After having my two children and leaving that abusive relationship, I moved to San Antonio, Texas, with my mom, kids, sister, and my two nephews, hoping for a fresh start. However, I soon found myself in another mentally abusive situation. I met new friends and got a job, and things were looking up. Due to my fear of dating, I preferred to spend time with friends, party, and focus on work. I started working at a customer service center, where I had the opportunity to make more friends. Even though we went out to clubs, I would turn down men's advances. After living with my sister for a few years, I found a place for myself, my mom, and my two kids.

ANOTHER ABUSIVE RELATIONSHIP

During this time, I dated several guys, but none of the relationships lasted until I met the father of my third child. We dated for a while, and everything seemed great until I got pregnant. However, things changed when I became pregnant. I discovered my kids father, who was my boyfriend at the time, had another woman pregnant. Their child and our child were born months apart. This revelation was heartbreaking and brought a deep sense of betrayal and confusion. After our baby was born, he became verbally abusive. I realized that I had repeated the pattern of being with the wrong men in my life.

Determined not to endure mistreatment again, I knew I had to end this relationship.

I thought, I have to get out of this relationship; it's not fruitful, and this is not someone I want to be with.

Feeling like I did in my first relationship, I once again vowed that no one would treat me poorly. So, I left him and decided I was done with dating, or so I thought. One night, while waiting for my friend by the exit of a club, a guy stood by the door staring at me. I prepared to confront him if he approached me with inappropriate talk. But he was a gentleman. He said all the right words. In the back of my mind, I was thinking, "What issues does he have?" I was hesitant at first, but I gave him a chance. We began dating, and he was great with my three kids. He started taking care of us, and after six months of dating, he popped the question with a beautiful ring and asked me to marry him. Excitedly, I said yes, and three months later, we were married.

SPIRITUAL AWAKENING

I attended cosmetology school, graduated, and started working at a salon. That's when my entire life began to change. I noticed a lady named Zonnie reading her Bible and became curious about what she was reading. It reminded me of a guy who used to come to the beauty school handing out Bible tracts, which I used to reject and throw away. Now, a year later, I found myself inquiring about the Lord!

Zonnie would share what she was reading and eventually invited me to her church. The first time I went, my husband and I both gave our lives to the Lord. From then on, we started attending church every Sunday. At this time my husband was in the Army, which often meant the possibility of moving to different locations, including foreign countries. My husband received orders to go Germany. Three months later he left ahead of us, because there was no housing available at the time. After three more months, I was able to join him in Germany, along with my mother and children.

We moved into a spacious five-bedroom home, thanks to the German economy that allowed everyone to have their own room. I met a woman who became my mentor. She resided downstairs and told me she had been praying for the family who would live there. It seemed like a divine setup from the Lord. She invited me to her church and introduced us to the pastors. As a result, we started attending church every Wednesday and Sunday.

BLOSSOMING IN GERMANY

Charlotte, my mentor, began teaching me how to pray and how to discern the voice of God for myself. I enthusiastically participated in women's retreats and conferences. I was fully invested in my spiritual journey! Eventually, I started working in a salon and, after a year, opened my own. I wondered how I could get a shampoo bowl and dryers to Germany, but it turned out that God had everything set up for me before I even knew Him. I was a babe in Christ, discovering new aspects of life and faith.

I met two German ladies who notified me of a salon owner named Klaus who was closing his shop and looking to sell everything. There were so many items that I couldn't take them all. My cup began to overflow with blessings. I managed to purchase an entire salon furniture set, which included hair dryers hanging from the ceiling, a shampoo bowl emerging from the floor, hair stations, rollers, and more, all for 800 euros. Truly, as the scripture says, "my cup runneth over" (Psalm 23:5).

My husband and I rented a moving truck and stored everything until I was ready to open my salon. The German ladies also helped me find a space in an apartment building, and the German landlord fixed it up and installed the shampoo bowls for me. Everything was falling into place, and it felt like the hand of the Lord was guiding me. I paid 800 euros a month for that space, and my business flourished, making over 1,000 euros a day. It became a great success. In my salon, I served a diverse clientele, including Nigerian queens, Turkish people, Africans, and Germans. Life felt abundant, and I enjoyed the fruits of my labor. I even bought a BMW X5 with cash and wanted for nothing. My success allowed me to take trips to Italy, Austria, Czechoslovakia, and Poland.

STRUGGLES AND FAITH

However, life took a turn when my husband was deployed to Iraq after 9/11. He worked late nights preparing for his deployment, and when the day came for him to leave, it was an incredibly sad time for me. Despite having my church family, business, and children, I felt abandoned and alone. My husband would share with me how difficult and frightening his experience was. Thankfully, our military support group formed a prayer group, and we began praying daily for the spouses in Iraq. Every day, I prayed for my husband's safe return, and a year later, he arrived home safe.

During this challenging time, my son Timothy ran into trouble at school for carrying a pocket knife while my husband was in Iraq. The principal wanted to expel him permanently, and I was still in the early stages of my walk with God. Thankfully, my mentor Charlotte prayed with us and helped navigate the situation. We had to appear in front of the commander and the head of the school to plead our case. It was a stressful moment, but we remained calm and composed. Ultimately, the truth came out: my son wasn't the one who brought the knife; it was another boy. Timothy was allowed to return to school after a 30-day suspension.

This experience reinforced my belief that the devil will never succeed in trying to destroy God's people. After my husband returned, we took a much-needed trip to Hawaii, visiting Spain and France before eventually returning to Germany. A few months later, we were baptized together, and our time in Germany ended as we were relocated to Fort Jackson, South Carolina.

POSTPARTUM DEPRESSION AND CHURCH HURT

After being stationed in South Carolina in 2004 and settling on post, we found a new church. I started working at a salon owned by the church, which was a nice change. However, I had to quit when I became pregnant. On August 8, 2005, I gave birth to my son, Uzziah. Initially, I was happy, but soon after, I began to feel different. I became deeply depressed, though I never sought medical help. Through much research, I now believe it was postpartum depression. I didn't want anything to do with my baby. I stopped attending church and spent most of my time lying in bed. My husband stepped up, taking care of Uzziah and managing everything else. I would breastfeed Uzziah, then hand him over to my husband for the rest of his care.

My husband and mom prayed for me constantly. One day, I woke up and decided I was going to church. During the service, there was an altar call, and I went forward for prayer. Something changed in me that day. Over the next few months, I gradually became more present for my son and regained my strength and joy. During this time, we had our first home built from the ground up, and everything seemed to be looking up. However, our lives took a challenging turn when my husband received orders to be stationed in South Korea.

During this time, things also changed at the church I attended. I experienced rejection, gossip, and betrayal, which deeply hurt both me and my daughter, especially when she became pregnant at 15 years old. It was a heartbreaking experience, but then I heard the Lord telling me it was time to leave that church. Before my husband returned, I followed that guidance and left the church. Some people criticized my decision, but I knew I had to obey God's voice. God's unconditional love blessed me and my family abundantly. Despite the challenges we faced, we were not cursed, and nothing stopped in our lives because we didn't follow man's protocol. God sees our hearts and knows our true motives. This decision led to more gossip and lies being spread about me. Despite the rumors, I knew deep down that I had made the right decision for myself and my family.

CHANGES AND CHALLENGES

After my husband returned home from Korea, he changed. He no longer wanted to attend church or serve God. I remembered a vision I had while he was in Korea, which seemed to have influenced his decision. I suggested that we go to church and seek prayer. He agreed, and during this time in South Carolina we started attending another church. I knew it would be short-lived because we had orders to go to Fort Carson in Colorado Springs. Still, during this period, my husband and I barely spoke to each other. I was preoccupied with everything that was happening, but I knew I needed to focus on pursuing God more than anything else. This was a challenging time for us, not only because of the strain in our relationship, but also because I discovered that my younger son was experiencing hearing loss after arriving in Colorado Springs. He needed surgery to get tubes in his ears for proper hearing. Balancing these challenges and earnestly seeking the Lord was incredibly difficult, but I felt His presence guiding me through each trial.

LOSS AND HEALING

Additionally, my mom was suffering from renal failure, and sadly, she passed away after two months. This entire process was emotionally overwhelming for me. I always believed that my mom would survive, as I thought a mother is supposed to be in your life forever, and it was difficult to accept that it was her time to go. Witnessing my mom lying in the hospital, helpless and barely able to move, I pleaded with God for her healing. I held onto hope, believing that she would recover.

During my time at the hospital, another young lady shared the room with us. Despite everything going on with my mom, God prompted me to pray for the young lady as well. At first, I hesitated, thinking I should solely focus on my mom's situation. However, the prompting persisted until I finally approached the young lady and inquired about her condition. She revealed she was there due to renal failure, just like my mom. I asked if I could pray for her, and she agreed. I left the hospital that day, but returned the following day to find that the young lady had miraculously left. The nurse informed me that she was remarkably better. This experience brought excitement, as I believed that if God had healed her, He would undoubtedly heal my mom too.

Unfortunately, my mom's health did not improve, and she eventually passed away. Her death was devastating for me, and I couldn't help but question why she wasn't healed. Despite my disappointment, I tried to move forward with life. However, I stopped praying for others' healing, even though I had seen the young lady experience a miraculous recovery. I felt that God wasn't listening to my prayers.

Years later, I heard that I was called to heal, but I initially dismissed this idea. Eventually, I confided in my mentor about my struggles. She mentioned that just because God didn't heal my mom, it didn't mean

He wouldn't heal me or others. This revelation struck a chord within me, and I allowed the Lord to heal the broken place in my heart.

I had never stopped to grieve, because I was angry at God for not healing my mom and taking her from me. However, I know my mom is in a better place now, free from pain and suffering. During this time, my daughter, who had been living with me, decided to return to South Carolina to be with her daughter Aniyah's father. Before she left, we had a bad argument, and she stormed out of the house. A week after arriving there, she was jailed for stabbing him. I believed this was a consequence of her disobedience toward me before she left. We had a bad argument, and she stormed out. When she called me from jail, she asked if I could get her out. I thought, "How can I help her after she was so disrespectful to me?"

As I prayed, I heard the Lord say, "Go get her now, or the enemy will devour her." I knew I needed to act quickly. Lacking the necessary funds, I reached out to my niece, who loaned me the money to bail her out and hire a good lawyer. We had to fly back and forth to South Carolina for court. She was facing 10 years in prison at 17 years old. I said, "The devil is a lie," and I began to pray. She was placed on probation and then got community service, which she only did one day, and was off probation. How does this work? God does not treat us as our sins deserve. I fasted and prayed every day to hear and be led by the Lord for my daughter's redemption.

It was the hand of the Lord upon my daughter; He loves us so much, even in our sin, that He reaches down into the miry clay and pulls us out from the clutches of satan. During this time, while my daughter was dealing with the legal situation in South Carolina, there was a custody issue with my granddaughter Aniyah. The other grandmother Aniyah's father's mother refused to give Aniyah back and insisted she would never return her. I went to the police station, and they said there was nothing they could do. So, I pondered and prayed; I remembered the Lord saying I would help raise my granddaughter, so I held onto those words. The next day, I called the police again and got a new person and explained the situation. The officer said to meet him there in 20 minutes. He instructed me to stay back from her house. The officer knocked on the door and ordered the person inside to release the child. The woman inside spoke, but her words were incomprehensible, like gibberish. The officer asked her to clarify and signaled for me to come forward. She handed over the child, and we left. Sadly, my granddaughter never saw her grandmother or father again.

I couldn't help but wonder who would lie and try to take someone's child. The devil is a liar, and my granddaughter was only two years old at that time. Now she is about to turn 17 and has been in my life ever since. I am grateful to God for that. He is a God who doesn't lie, and when He says something, it settles it, no matter how it may appear. I've learned to value my sanity and freedom more than anything else. Listening to God, not man, and obeying His commands is crucial. I put my trust in God, for He will guide me to where I am meant to be. He never leaves us nor forsakes us. My daughter has reached a place of some forgiveness, and I've taught my kids and grandkids to forgive others, even when they deceive, or act mean. I encourage them to release those people to God and let Him handle things with His grace and mercy.

I thank God for always being mindful of us, even when others may not be. The enemy tries to burden us with negative, self-defeating thoughts and pushes us toward unforgiveness. However, it's essential to see people the way God sees them, as it will help us in our walk with God.

LEARNING RESILIENCE

During this time, I also became embarrassed about my son's speech difficulties and multiple surgeries. You may wonder, "That is your son. How can you think like this?" But I couldn't help feeling that God was punishing me through my son's struggles. Through these trials, I learned the importance of resilience and unwavering faith. My son's journey taught me that even in the darkest times, there is hope. His courage and determination inspired me to keep pushing forward, no matter the obstacles.

For parents facing similar challenges, I want to share that you are not alone. Seek support from your community, lean on your faith, and never lose hope. The road may be tough, but with love, patience, and perseverance, you can overcome anything.

Pursuing God

In an effort to find solace and strength, I started attending the Deborah Company meetings every Tuesday. I took my son with me after he got out of school. I joined the inner healing team at my church and began learning about intercessory prayer. I also attended deliverance schools and dream classes. My pursuit of God helped me maintain my sanity after losing my mom.

Three years later, God led me to attend Nazarene Bible College. There, I learned how to study God's word and exegete scriptures, meaning to interpret them. My professors encouraged me to bring healing to other students by being vulnerable and sharing my story of contracting a STD from my was my first child's father. This sharing had a powerful impact, as other students thanked me for revealing that they were not alone in experiencing similar challenges.

I realized the importance of sharing our stories, as it brings healing to God's people. As Revelation 12:11 says that We overcome by the words of our testimonies. By sharing my testimony, I was able to connect with others on a deeper level and contribute to their healing journeys.

Legal Struggles and Triumph

After the personal upheavals, another challenge arose, not uncommon in situations of family strain. There was a legal attempt to challenge my custody of Michaeala, my third child, instigated by influences that did not have our family's best interest at heart. This legal action forced us to secure a lawyer and face the uncertainties of the court system. It was a time filled with anxiety, but I clung to memories of past difficulties from which we had emerged stronger.

We prepared for the court proceedings, which were to take place in San Antonio, Texas, where Michaela was born. The process was nerve-wracking, but on the day of the hearing, I felt a newfound boldness. This strength was not my own; it was as if I was being fortified by divine support. I entered the courtroom with a firm conviction that truth and justice would prevail, despite the web of untruths we were up against.

In the end, the court recognized the stability and love I provided for Michaela, and she remained in my custody. Another hearing was scheduled, but I received a strong impression that I did not need to attend, as the jurisdiction did not extend to compel our presence further. Following this guidance, the issue was surprisingly not pursued further.

This situation taught me that even when the devil schemes, God has a way of turning situations around for His purposes. It reinforced the lesson that in every life storm, we must anchor ourselves in faith and trust that God's plans are for our welfare and protection. Hebrews 6:19: "We have this hope as an anchor for the soul, firm and secure. It enters the inner sanctuary behind the curtain."

Chapter 3

BETRAYED TRUST

Ephesians 5:25 "Husbands, love your wives, just as Christ loved the Church and gave himself up for her." (NIV)

During this period, I faced a devastating blow of betrayal that deeply shook me. The discovery of betrayal in a close relationship left me shocked and emotionally spiraling. I struggled with the pain and hurt, which burrowed deeper each day, prompting a multitude of questions about trust and loyalty.

To address the challenges in our relationship, we agreed that counseling was necessary. The sessions initially intensified my emotions, but they gradually began to provide some solace and understanding. My husband who betrayed me repeatedly expressed remorse and a desire for forgiveness, claiming no intention to cause hurt. Initially, I blamed myself, questioning if I could have somehow prevented the betrayal.

However, as we continued counseling, I learned that the responsibility for the betrayal did not lie with me. The counselor introduced various exercises and techniques aimed at rebuilding trust and strengthening our relationship. Although I felt peace after the sessions, the journey back to trust was fraught with setbacks, especially when old grievances resurfaced.

My close friends played a crucial role during this time, helping me to avoid sinking into self-pity. My emotions were tumultuous, oscillating between forgiveness and resentment. There were days when the pain seemed insurmountable, but slowly, insights gained during counseling began to take root.

One morning, overcome by emotions, I found myself crying uncontrollably. To provide comfort, my husband began to pray for me earnestly and arranged for us to meet with our counselor. These gestures marked a turning point in our healing process.

We both recognized the need to forgive and move forward, not just for the sake of our relationship, but for our individual peace. During this challenging time, I discovered that external influences had exacerbated our issues, with some people having motives to see our relationship fail. This realization helped me to understand the broader dynamics at play and the spiritual warfare involved.

In facing such trials, we must continually seek divine guidance and apply spiritual discernment. It is essential to remember that God is in the business of redemption and healing. He calls us to see others

COURAGE: A REDEMPTION STORY

through His eyes of grace and to fight against the divisive tactics of the enemy.

Reflecting on this experience, I learned the importance of guarding my heart and relationships and the power of forgiveness and healing. I severed ties with those who proved toxic, finding freedom and peace in trusting God's plan.

THE SPIRITUAL BATTLE FOR MARRIAGE

Satan hates marriage and he hates the covenant it represents. He wants nothing more than to destroy your marriage. You have to fight for your marriage and stand up to the devil when he comes against you. Remember, marriage is meant to be a three-strand cord, and what God has put together, let no man put asunder.

As Ecclesiastes 4:12 (NIV) says, "Though one may be overpowered, two can defend themselves. A cord of three strands is not quickly broken." And Mark 10:9 (NIV) reminds us, "Therefore what God has joined together, let no one separate."

I remember my mentor once told me, "You are called to marriages." At the time, I thought, "Not with the way my marriage is going." But now, I see that what I have been through can actually help others in their marriages. We are not perfect, but God is.

I was once told that I would be taken care of if I got a divorce. However, if you stand for righteousness, your entire family can be saved. It was my choice, but I decided to give my marriage another try. There were many times I wanted to divorce my husband. In my anger, I even filled out the divorce papers. But then I heard the Lord say, "Do you want your marriage or not? If you stay, I can help you. If you don't, then that's your choice, but I'm here for you no matter what."

I thank God for a trusted friend who called out this behavior. It is essential to be wise and prayerful before confronting such behaviors. Understanding the spiritual implications and being grounded in prayer can prepare you to address these issues effectively.

Practical Steps for Strengthening Your Marriage

- **Prayer and Devotion**: Pray together daily and share devotional times to strengthen your spiritual bond.
- **Seeking Counsel**: Seek guidance from trusted mentors, pastors, or marriage counselors to work through difficult times.
- **Communication Skills**: Improve communication skills by practicing active listening, expressing feelings calmly, and using "I" statements.
- **Acts of Service**: Perform simple acts of service and kindness towards each other to build a culture of mutual respect and love.

PERSONAL TESTIMONY AND ENCOURAGEMENT

This experience taught me that God is always with us, no matter how difficult the situation. Standing for righteousness in your marriage can lead to healing and redemption for your entire family. It is a choice, but it's one that can lead to immense growth and blessing.

Remember Romans 8:28: "And we know that in all things God works for the good of those who love him, who have been called according to his purpose."

Additionally, Ephesians 5:33 emphasizes the need for love and respect in marriage: "However, each one of you also must love his wife as he loves himself, and the wife must respect her husband."

Standing firm in your marriage is not just about enduring the tough times, but growing through them. God's promises are true, and His faithfulness endures forever. Let your marriage be a testament to His glory and grace.

Wives, we must pray for our husbands every chance that we get, as he is the head of the home. You must bring the cross into every situation you face in life. Understand what tree you are eating from, as quoted by Steve Chua, a popular bible teacher. . God is in the redemption business, so do not allow the devil to plant lies in your head about your marriage, husband, or children.

I have been betrayed by friends whom I trusted—or at least, I thought they were my friends. When you confide in a friend, and they go on to repeat everything you say to their friends or significant other, and it eventually gets back to you, that is not true friendship. I was discussing this person with my sister and mentioned that I thought this person would have my back. In response, my sister described this person as a pendulum, constantly swinging back and forth. One minute, they are supportive, and the next, they are speaking negatively about you to others. I was astonished because this description perfectly matched how this person behaved.

Eventually, I had to cut off all communication with this individual. It was not an easy decision, but it brought me a sense of freedom that I had never experienced before. This hurt me, just like what my husband did to me. People can be awful, but it is essential to keep your eyes on the Lord. He is the one who will heal you and help you through every betrayal in your life. Remember, He will never stop fighting for us.

Rose in the desert

THE ROSE POEM

The rose untold was never bold.

Lost in deep feelings, like a lost sheep

In the midst of every disappointment, in my heap of mourning.

I started as a seed in my mother's womb.

The pruning began as I started to bloom.

I saw a bright light. I kept the perfect climate,

As I began to germinate in my dormancy to stay private.

I thought I could never stay quiet.

The enemy tried to silence me.

I said, "I'm a child of the King."

I am fragrant like a rose that became bold,

Vibrant to behold, His beauty untold.

Chapter 4

THE POWER OF FORGIVENESS

Genesis 50:20 "But as for you, you meant evil against me, but God meant it for good."

Forgiveness is deeply challenging yet profoundly transformative, as epitomized by the biblical story of Joseph. Despite the betrayal and hardships he faced, Joseph's journey through jealousy, false accusations, and ultimate reconciliation illustrates the profound power of forgiveness. He famously said in Genesis 50:20, "But as for you, you meant evil against me, but God meant it for good." This statement underscores a pivotal biblical truth: God can transform our deepest wounds and darkest moments into opportunities for grace and growth.

PERSONAL STRUGGLES WITH FORGIVENESS

During my relationship with my children's father in East St. Louis, I had an abortion. At that time, it was normal in our community to have abortions and discuss them openly. My older sister took me to get the procedure. I felt a deep sense of shame when I discovered I was pregnant again, especially since my daughter hadn't even celebrated her first birthday. After moving to Colorado, I joined a church that had a strong mission to stop abortions. It was then explained to me how God does not want us to have abortions. Through this journey, I finally sought inner healing and forgave my sister, my mother, and the doctor for this painful decision.

I wish I had someone to talk to and a support system back then. In total, I had three abortions. Despite my past, I thank God for His grace and mercy towards me, and for being a forgiving God.

OVERCOMING SHAME

After I learned how wrong abortions were, I couldn't believe I had done this. I struggled with shame over what I had done and with people judging me after they found out. These feelings lingered for years, affecting my self-esteem and mental health.

If you are struggling with the aftermath of an abortion and have been holding it in, know that there are many organizations out there to help you, and you can also talk to someone you trust. Psalms 34:18 says, "The Lord is close to the brokenhearted and saves those who are crushed in spirit." And 1 John 1:9 reminds us, "If we confess our sins, He is faithful and just to forgive us our sins and to cleanse us from all unrighteousness."

CREATING A SAFE SPACE

It is crucial that we create a safe space for open discussions about abortion. By being open and honest, we can provide support, reduce stigma, and help others make informed decisions. No one should have to keep this bottled inside and feel alone.

This experience has taught me to become stronger and be more empathetic. I now understand the importance of compassion, both for myself and others. No more being judgmental. My faith has deepened, and I am more committed than ever to helping others find redemption and peace. Remember, no matter what you've gone through, there is always hope for new beginnings. God's grace and mercy are sufficient for us all. He is always standing with open arms, loving and forgiving us. You are never alone.

THE ACT OF FORGIVENESS

The act of forgiveness, as encouraged in Ephesians 4:31-32, which urges us to "Get rid of all bitterness, rage and anger, brawling and slander, along with every form of malice," and to "Be kind and compassionate to one another, forgiving each other, just as in Christ God forgave you," is not just a moral directive but a path to spiritual and emotional liberation. Forgiving others allows us to break free from the cycle of pain and resentment, opening our hearts to unconditional love and compassion.

FORGIVENESS IN ACTION

Forgiveness chart

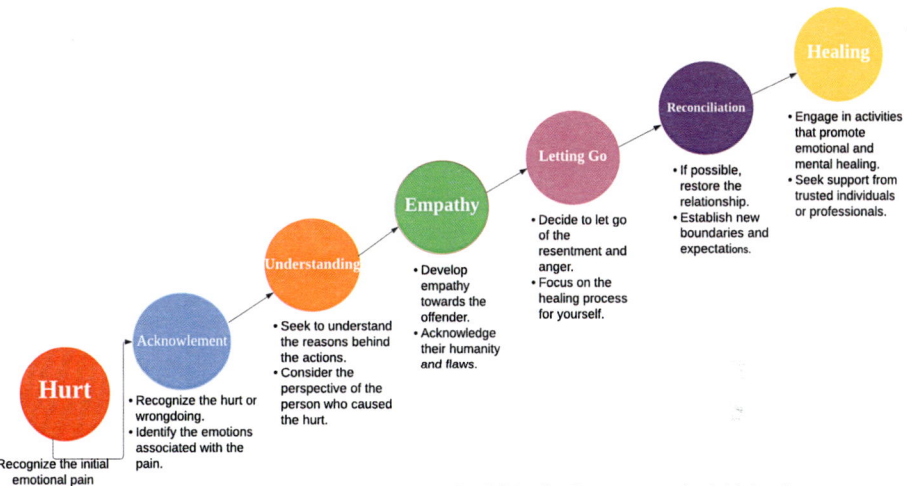

- **Red (Hurt)** - Represents the initial pain and suffering.
- **Biblical Meaning:** Blood, sacrifice, and redemption.
- **Blue (Acknowledgment)** - Reflects recognition and acceptance of emotions.
- **Biblical Meaning:** Heaven, divine revelation, and spiritual understanding.
- **Orange (Understanding)** - Symbolizes the process of understanding the reasons behind the hurt.
- **Biblical Meaning:** Represents fire and purification.
- **Green (Empathy)** - Represents growth, healing, and the development of empathy.
- **Biblical Meaning:** Life, renewal, and healing.
- **Pink (Letting Go)** - Suggests compassion and the act of releasing anger.
- **Biblical Meaning:** Joy, gratitude, and love.
- **Purple (Reconciliation)** - Reflects the noble act of restoring relationships.
- **Biblical Meaning:** Royalty, priesthood, and the Kingdom of God.
- **Yellow (Healing)** - Represents the final stage of healing and wholeness.
- **Biblical Meaning:** Glory, faith, and anointing.

Childhood Experiences and Racism

I remember every year we would go to Monks Mounds in Cahokia on holidays—Memorial Day, Fourth of July, and Labor Day. One day, as we were enjoying ourselves, a truck drove by, and someone yelled, "Go home, n*****s." My stepdad responded, "You go home, honky." As a little girl, this incident stuck with me, and growing up, I continued to see racism, even in 2024.

I always had thoughts about Caucasian people and remembered being told to look them in the eye so they wouldn't think I was lying. As I got older, I questioned why I had to prove myself to them. Why did I have to look them in the eye?

Healing from Racism

During a period of transition, a pastor advised me to join an apostolic prophetic church, saying it was pivotal for my calling. She looked up churches for me on Elijah's List, and I found an event happening at Dutch Sheets church. I attended the event and heard the Lord say,

"This is where I want you planted, huh? This church has white people in it" but nevertheless, I knew God had my best interest at heart. From there, God placed me around five anointed women of God, one of whom became my mentor. It was through these relationships that God began to heal me from the church hurts I had experienced in my previous church.

When I started attending this mostly white church, I began to learn that not all white people are racist and that they are not out to get me.

I learned to forgive white people, because they are not all racist, and I began to form deep relationships with them. However, I was never sat down and talked to about racism; it was something I observed and heard about, but was never taught.

God loves all people and is not racist, so why should we be? I've learned that there are still racist people in this world. I pray that hate and racism can be redeemed through forgiveness. Forgiving is God doing a deep work inside of us. He wants us to love and forgive others as many times as it takes. Matthew 18:21-22 (NIV): "Then Peter came to Jesus and asked, 'Lord, how many times shall I forgive my brother or sister who sins against me? Up to seven times?' Jesus answered, 'I tell you, not seven times, but seventy-seven times.'" I thank God that I can forgive others as He forgives us.

PERSONAL JOURNEY OF FORGIVENESS

However, forgiveness is not always about others; it often involves a deep personal journey. There have been numerous times in my life when I needed to seek forgiveness, and each instance taught me more about the importance of moving forward. Holding onto unforgiveness can act like a poison, affecting your physical health as well as your emotional and spiritual well-being. For example, the stress of my unresolved anger and bitterness once caused my thyroid gland to become overactive, leading to significant weight loss and hair loss. This personal health crisis highlighted the physical toll that emotional burdens can exact.

Isaiah 1:18 offers a divine invitation to reconciliation: "Come now, let us settle the matter," says the LORD. "Though your sins are like scarlet, they shall be as white as snow; though they are red as crimson, they shall be like wool." This scripture reassures us of God's boundless capacity for forgiveness, emphasizing that no matter what has been done to us—or what we have done—redemption is always possible.

FORGIVING ONESELF AND GOD

It is also crucial to recognize that forgiveness can sometimes involve forgiving oneself or even God. Many of us, me included, have felt betrayed by life's circumstances, or by God's seeming inaction in the face of our suffering. I had to confront these feelings of anger toward God, which was a profound and challenging process. Acknowledging this hidden resentment was the first step towards healing and forgiving myself and God. Remember, it is not God's fault when terrible things happen—our world is complex, and suffering often arises from many sources, including human free will.

THOROUGH FORGIVENESS

Moreover, forgiveness must be thorough. A superficial declaration of forgiveness is not enough if we continue to harbor negative thoughts or feelings. Hebrews 12:15 warns, "See to it that no one falls short of the grace of God and that no bitter root grows up to cause trouble and defile many." This passage teaches us to be vigilant against the subtle growth of bitterness, which can quietly take root deep within our hearts.

Forgiveness is not merely an emotional release, but also a commitment to renewing our minds and spirits. If thoughts of past hurts still dominate our minds or if seeing someone still sparks anger, we might need to reassess our hearts for lingering unforgiveness. True forgiveness aligns with virtues that are "true, honest, just, pure, lovely, and of good report." Giving up your right to be right.

CONCLUSION

In closing, forgiveness is a journey that requires constant attention and effort. It involves everyone and everything that might have caused us pain—from family members and friends to life itself. By choosing forgiveness, we not only obey God's command, but also free ourselves to live fully, unencumbered by the weight of past grievances.

Part 2:

The Miracle -
What Father Did

Chapter 5

HEALING FROM WITHIN

Inner healing is a transformative process where God mends the broken areas of our hearts. It is about allowing God to reach deep into our being to heal wounds that we sometimes do not even recognize we carry. As Revelation 21:4 poignantly reminds us, "He will wipe every tear from their eyes. There will be no more death or mourning or crying or pain, for the old order of things has passed away." This verse not only promises the removal of physical suffering, but also the deep emotional and spiritual healing that comes from God.

There was a time in my life when the weight of my challenges felt so overwhelming that I contemplated ending my life. It is a stark reminder that even the strongest among us can find themselves in moments of profound despair. In those dark times, it is crucial to remember that God knows our end from our beginning. He sees not just what we are, but what we can become.

During the journey of inner healing, God prunes us, cutting away the parts of our lives that do not align with His purpose. This process can be painful and challenging. Jeremiah 17:9 tells us, "The heart is deceitful above all things and desperately wicked: who can know it?" I had never considered that suicidal thoughts reflected a deeper spiritual malady. It is a stark example of how destructive thoughts can lurk in our hearts without our conscious awareness.

In those moments, God wants to cleanse us of all impurities—what the Bible refers to as 'dross,' which is considered worthless. He aims to purify us, making us beautiful inside and out, and remove any barriers to our spiritual growth. The realization that God spared my life during my lowest point made it clear that He was not done with me. His plans are to prosper us, not to harm us, to give us hope and a future.

One particularly poignant moment of inner healing involved forgiving those who had hurt me deeply—my husband, who I felt had caused much of my pain, and friends who turned out to be insincere. Through this, I learned that harboring unforgiveness was like walking with a heavy, invisible chain. Psalm 23:7 became a personal anthem for me: "You are my hiding place; You, Lord, protect me from trouble; You surround me with songs of deliverance." God's presence offered me a fortress of comfort and strength, shielding me from the storms of betrayal and disappointment.

As I was going through inner healing, a painful memory surfaced: I was abused at 19 by my kids' uncle. I couldn't believe that I had blocked this out for over 30 years. During this time, I would see and talk to him, normalizing the experience, which was heartbreaking to realize. I believe God brought this up as I was writing my book on redemption.

Confronting this memory allowed me to truly forgive him and face my own pain. I didn't know how my kids or my husband would react, but my main purpose was to forgive and allow God to heal me. Reflecting on this, I realized why I struggled to relate to men, to say no, or to report the incident to the police.

This has been an emotional inner healing journey, and I pray that anyone who has experienced a similar incident understands that it's not your fault. Report the perpetrator to the authorities, no matter who they are. Being free is redemption in itself.

Inner healing also involves confronting and letting go of generational sins and patterns that may have influenced our lives. It is about recognizing that Satan, described in the Bible as the prince of the air, has no rightful place in our lives. We must actively surrender every part of ourselves to God's healing process. This surrender involves acknowledging that we might still have areas in our lives in need of God's touch, just as Isaiah 44:22 reassures us, "I have swept away your offenses like a cloud; your sins are like the morning mist. Return to me, for I have redeemed you."

Throughout my journey, I have learned that inner healing is not always instantaneous; it can be like peeling an onion, layer by layer, or like removing the petals of a rose, one at a time. Each session of inner healing has revealed new areas in need of God's healing hand. I have come to realize that no matter how perfect we might think we are, God always sees more potential, more purity, more of His image in us.

This ongoing process is crucial for us to bear fruit and truly reflect the beauty and fragrance of Christ. As we continue to engage in inner healing, we become the embodiment of the divine fragrance that God desires in His presence—a sweet-smelling savor that is pleasing to Him. Inner healing, though it may be painful, is worth every moment, for it leads us to become who God has created us to be, full of life and free from the past's shadows.

Chapter 6

FREEDOM UNLEASHED

Sinkholes

UNDERSTANDING SPIRITUAL SINKHOLES

A sinkhole represents a sudden and devastating collapse of the ground, much like the spiritual collapses we face when we harbor offenses. These breaches of spiritual law—whether through illegal acts or personal resentments—create voids in our spiritual landscape that can dangerously undermine our foundation. Just as natural sinkholes form from acidic conditions eroding underground cavities, our spiritual sinkholes develop from unaddressed sins and emotional wounds, leading to a precarious state where one's spirit can collapse under the weight of unresolved issues. These spiritual collapses are not only deep and wide but are also filled with the debris of pride, envy, and insecurity.

SINKHOLES OF LIFE

Just like sinkholes can appear suddenly and without warning, life's challenges—such as loss, betrayal, illness, or financial hardship—can catch us off guard, leaving us feeling destabilized and unsure of our footing.

These moments remind us of the need to remain rooted in our faith. When life's sinkholes appear, we must turn to God for stability, much like how a solid foundation prevents a sinkhole from causing greater damage.

Sinkholes can symbolize the deep emotional despair we sometimes experience, where it feels like we're being pulled into a dark place with no way out.

Psalm 40:2 speaks of God lifting us out of the "miry pit" and setting us on solid ground. In times of emotional despair, we can trust that God will rescue us from these sinkholes, giving us a firm place to stand.

Holding onto unforgiveness can create a spiritual sinkhole, slowly eroding our peace and joy until we find ourselves trapped in bitterness.

Forgiveness is the key to preventing and escaping this sinkhole. By choosing to forgive, we allow God to fill in the gaps and restore us to solid ground.

When we become complacent in our spiritual walk, neglecting prayer, worship, or studying God's word, we may find ourselves gradually sinking into a spiritual void.

Staying vigilant in our faith and maintaining a close relationship with God is like regularly inspecting our foundation to ensure no sinkholes are forming beneath the surface.

Over time, compromising on our values or principles can lead to a slow erosion of our moral and spiritual foundation, eventually resulting in a sinkhole that can cause a major collapse in our lives.

Maintaining integrity and staying true to God's word helps us avoid these moral and spiritual sinkholes, keeping our foundation strong and secure.

Life's sinkholes can be frightening and destabilizing, but they also serve as a call to depend on God more fully. Just as engineers study and reinforce the ground to prevent sinkholes, we can reinforce our spiritual foundation through prayer, worship, and the study of God's Word. When we encounter these sinkholes, we can trust that God will lift us out, set us on solid ground, and help us navigate the challenges of life with His guidance and strength.

We need deliverance to persevere. Deliverance is a powerful spiritual process where God frees us from anything that binds us—anything that is not of Him. Isaiah 43:18-19 beautifully captures the essence of this process: "Forget the former things; do not dwell on the past. See, I am doing a new thing! Now it springs up; do you not perceive it? I am making a way in the wilderness and streams in the wasteland." These verses promise that God is actively working to transform our lives, guiding us out of our personal wilderness and into new, life-giving paths.

PERSONAL EXPERIENCE WITH DELIVERANCE

In my own life, deliverance has been a transformative experience, fundamentally changing the way I live and perceive the world. It began with the challenging task of renouncing old wounds and bindings—some of which I was aware of, and others that had subtly influenced me without my conscious knowledge. Many of these issues, such as generational curses, past traumas, and deep-seated fears, had kept me from living in the fullness of my identity in Christ.

The process of deliverance involves acknowledging these bindings and actively rejecting them. To renounce, in this context, means to refuse to follow, obey, or recognize these negative influences any further. It is a firm declaration that you are choosing a different path—the path God has set for you.

During my time as a deliverance minister at Ram Ministries in Colorado Springs, Colorado, I had the privilege of seeing God's power firsthand.

I witnessed people being freed from demonic oppression, sickness, poverty, and deep emotional scars. It was incredibly moving to see individuals transform before my eyes—becoming lighter, brighter, and more alive as they shed the weights that had long held them down.

Consider the metamorphosis of a butterfly, which symbolizes profound transformation. Just as a caterpillar becomes a butterfly, emerging beautifully and uniquely formed, so too does each person who undergoes deliverance. This transformation is not merely an external change but a complete renewal from the inside out, aligning with Romans 12:2 which calls us not to conform to this world, but to be transformed by the renewing of our minds. This renewal allows us to discern God's good, pleasing, and perfect will.

Metamorphosis of a butterfly

RECOGNIZING AND CLAIMING PROMISES

Deliverance can lead to recognizing and claiming the promise found in Isaiah 61:7, "Instead of your shame you will receive a double portion, and instead of disgrace you will rejoice in your inheritance. And so, you will inherit a double portion in your land, and everlasting joy will be yours." God doesn't just restore; He multiplies. He replaces our pain with joy and our losses with an inheritance that far surpasses our past sufferings.

This journey isn't always easy. It requires facing parts of ourselves that we might prefer to leave hidden. However, the freedom it brings is worth every moment of struggle. As we walk through deliverance, we shed the old and embrace the new, allowing God to fully realize the beautiful vision He has for each of our lives. We become like those butterflies—each different in color, size, and shape—each reflecting the unique beauty of God's creation.

PRACTICAL STEPS TO DELIVERANCE

Freedom

RECOGNIZING AND OVERCOMING THE JEZEBEL SPIRIT

In my journey of inner healing and spiritual growth, I encountered the concept of the Jezebel spirit. This demonic influence is named after Queen Jezebel in the Bible, known for her manipulation, control, and deceit. I began to see how this spirit could subtly influence relationships, particularly marriages.

RECOGNIZING THE SIGNS

A Jezebel spirit often manifests through:

- **Manipulation and Control**: Attempts to dominate or control the spouse, often through emotional manipulation or subtle coercion.
- **Deception and Lies**: Spreading falsehoods or creating confusion to maintain control.
- **Undermining Authority**: Disrespecting or undermining the spouse's authority or leadership in the family.

I realized that some of my behaviors, influenced by past hurts and generational patterns, aligned with these traits. For instance, arguing with my husband and putting his clothes out of the house was a form of control and manipulation that echoed the Jezebel spirit's influence. In a particularly heated moment, I even ripped our marriage license and threw my ring. These actions were symbolic of the deep disrespect and control issues I was struggling with.

A TURNING POINT

One day, during an argument, my son said, "I'm tired of hearing y'all argue." At first, I thought, "Who is he talking to?" But then I realized he was right. My children had been watching me argue with my husband, and it struck me how much they had been affected by it. My husband recently asked me, "Why did you talk to me like that and disrespect me?" His question made me reflect deeply on my actions and the negative patterns I had allowed to take root in our marriage.

During this period of my behavior, my husband confided that he had emotionally checked out of the marriage. The lack of effective communication had created a chasm between us. While this is no excuse for any betrayal that may have occurred, had we known how to communicate better, we might have averted such pain and misunderstanding.

I thank God for a trusted friend who called out this behavior. It is essential to be wise and prayerful before confronting such behaviors. Understanding the spiritual implications and being grounded in prayer can prepare you to address these issues effectively.

BREAKING FREE

To break free from the Jezebel spirit's influence, I had to undertake a few crucial steps:

- **Acknowledgment**: Recognizing and admitting the presence of this influence in my behavior was the first step.
- **Repentance**: Seeking God's forgiveness and repenting for allowing such behavior to take root in my marriage.
- **Inner Healing**: Undergoing inner healing to address the root causes of these behaviors, such as past traumas and generational patterns.
- **Spiritual Warfare**: Engaging in spiritual warfare through prayer, fasting, and the application of scripture to break the stronghold of the Jezebel spirit.

PRACTICAL STEPS FOR COUPLES

For couples facing similar challenges, here are some practical steps to consider:

- **Prayer Together**: Pray together regularly, asking God to reveal and remove any negative influences in your marriage.
- **Open Communication**: Maintain open and honest communication, addressing issues before they escalate into manipulation or control.
- **Seek Counsel**: Don't hesitate to seek counsel from trusted Christian leaders or counselors who can provide guidance and support.
- **Forgiveness**: Practice forgiveness, both seeking and granting it, to heal wounds and restore trust.

In practical terms, deliverance for me meant facing the deep-seated issues of depression, sadness, and loneliness that I hadn't fully acknowledged before. Once I faced these issues, I was surprised to learn how they manifested in ways I hadn't realized, affecting my daily life and relationships. Through prayer and surrender at the altar, I found freedom from these emotional burdens.

Deliverance is an ongoing process, a journey of being continually woven into the tapestry of God's love, where every detail of our lives is interconnected and purposed for good as stated in Romans 8:28. It's about becoming who God designed us to be, fully aligned with Him, thriving in every aspect of life. This alignment includes overcoming any physical ailments or emotional scars, as I experienced with my son's ear problems, which God also is healing, reminding me of His deep love and care for us.

In every session of deliverance, in every prayer of freedom, we see God's handiwork, His desire to bring us out of bondage into glorious freedom. As Psalm 77:14 proclaims, He is the God who works wonders, continually showing His power and love, ready to topple any stronghold that opposes His will for our lives.

Chapter 7

LEARNING TO WALK

Clear Path

After witnessing numerous spiritual encounters, I felt compelled to deepen my understanding of the divine. I eagerly enrolled in various classes focused on deliverance, hearing the voice of God, and dream interpretation. My past had not provided a positive representation of God, and I was determined to reshape this perception by equipping myself with knowledge and seeking the anointing necessary to fulfill my calling.

The God I came to know through these studies was vastly different from the judgmental figure I had been introduced to in earlier religious experiences. He was not concerned with controlling my actions or dictating my appearance; instead, He offered unconditional love and guidance. This realization both surprised and infuriated me, as I reflected on the ungodly behavior I had endured within the church. Yet, through each enlightening encounter, God peeled back layers of deception, aligning my steps with His word that promises, "The steps of a good man are ordered by the Lord."

As I continued to grow in my spiritual journey, I was surrounded by true men and women of God who provided support and encouragement. This nurturing environment was free from the controlling dynamics I had previously known. It was a place where I could thrive, leading intercessory prayers and feeling a profound connection with like-minded believers.

God blessed me with mentors, starting with my first mentor in Germany, who helped me understand that my life was securely held in His hands. Through spiritual warfare and the classes I attended, I learned to speak boldly against negative influences affecting me and my family. I reclaimed what the enemy had stolen and deepened my engagement in worship and effective prayer. I became involved in prophetic groups, praying not just for personal growth, but for lands, nations, and governments, aligning my actions with God's broader purposes.

Furthering my education at Bible college, I honed my ability to interpret God's word accurately, avoiding the pitfalls of taking scriptures out of context. Every class was a step towards understanding the vastness of God's grace and the depth of His plans for me.

COURAGE IN ACTION

My journey has also been marked by moments of profound courage, much like Esther's story in the Bible. She displayed remarkable bravery by intervening to save her people, a reminder that God calls us to be both brave and faithful. This courage was mirrored in my own life when I decided to search for my biological father and, subsequently, other family members I had never met.

Finding my father's obituary online and discovering I had siblings was a bittersweet moment filled with a mix of anticipation and fear. With my husband's support, we reached out to my sister. To my relief and joy, she was not only aware of me, but was also receptive to building a relationship. This marked the beginning of a new chapter in my family life, where I connected with siblings, nieces, and nephews I had never known. Our relationship grew quickly, bonded by shared blood and stories, and soon felt as if it had always existed.

The courage to reach out to these new family members was a pivotal moment in my life, showing me that God's timing is perfect, and His plans are often bigger than we can see. What the enemy intended for separation and pain in our family, God transformed into an opportunity for unity and love.

In every challenge, whether it was the custody battle for my granddaughter or standing against spiritual attacks on my family, God reminded me of the power of His presence. He reassured me that some battles were for me to fight, while others were for Him to handle. Learning to discern this difference was crucial.

Through it all, God continually equips us with courage and faith, enabling us to face trials with a steadfast heart and a clear mind. As Deuteronomy 31:6 urges us, "Be strong and of good courage. Do not be afraid or terrified because of them, for the Lord your God goes with you; he will never leave you nor forsake you." This is not just a call to bravery, but a divine command to trust in God's eternal strength and justice.

PRACTICAL ADVICE FOR SPIRITUAL GROWTH

I encourage you to seek out classes and mentorship, but make sure to pray about it first. God will lead you, just as He leads His people. Seek God on how to engage in spiritual warfare and prayer. God knows all things; He knows how He wants you to pray and how to actively engage in spiritual warfare. Now, when a situation arises, I ask God how to proceed. We don't want to waste time engaging in frivolous warfare or prayer.

For example, when my family faced a severe financial crisis, I sought God's guidance on how to pray and act. Instead of succumbing to fear, I asked God for wisdom. Through prayer, He led me to resources and opportunities that I hadn't considered. This experience taught me the importance of seeking God's direction in every aspect of life.

Another instance was when my son faced multiple surgeries due to hearing issues. Initially, I felt overwhelmed and unsure of how to pray effectively for his healing. I sought God's guidance, and He directed me to specific scriptures and prayers. I also reached out to my church community for support and intercession. Through persistent prayer and trusting in God's plan, my son's surgeries were successful, and his hearing improved significantly. This taught me the power of community prayer and the importance of seeking God's will in times of crisis.

ENCOURAGEMENT AND HOPE

For those who may feel overwhelmed by their spiritual journey, remember that you are not alone. It is essential to remain patient and persistent in seeking God's will and growing in faith. There will be challenges and moments of doubt, but God's presence is constant. Philippians 4:6-7 reminds us, "Do not be anxious about anything, but in every situation, by prayer and petition, with thanksgiving, present your requests to God. And the peace of God, which transcends all understanding, will guard your hearts and your minds in Christ Jesus."

Embrace each step of your journey with the assurance that God's plans for you are good. Trust in His timing, and lean on the support of a faith community. Jeremiah 29:11 reassures us, "For I know the plans I have for you, declares the Lord, plans to prosper you and not to harm you, plans to give you hope and a future."

CONCLUSION

The journey of spiritual equipping is ongoing, a lifetime of learning and growing in faith. It involves embracing the teachings of scripture, understanding God's voice, and applying these lessons to real-world challenges. Equipped with knowledge, anointed by the Holy Spirit, and guided by profound courage, we can navigate the complexities of life while fulfilling the divine purposes set before us.

Part 3:

How My Fathered Life Looks Today

Chapter 8

BLOSSOMING ANEW

Wisdom Precious Jewels

WISDOM: THE PRECIOUS JEWELS

Wisdom is likened to a precious jewel, a treasure that God bestows upon us. As Proverbs 4:7 (NASB) wisely advises, "The beginning of wisdom is: Acquire wisdom; and with your acquiring, get understanding." This proverb emphasizes the active pursuit necessary to obtain wisdom, highlighting that it involves both acquisition and understanding, much like treasuring a valuable possession.

In our daily lives, we are continually faced with decisions that require wisdom. Just as we protect our most cherished possessions, we must also safeguard the wisdom that God grants us. It is essential to cherish this divine wisdom, treating it as we would a dear friend or a beloved spouse. It is this depth of value and commitment to God's wisdom that shapes our lives, guiding our actions and decisions.

However, earthly wisdom often suggests we follow our instincts, which can be misleading as the heart can deceive us, as stated in Jeremiah 17:9. In contrast, godly wisdom is an invaluable treasure, akin to a chest filled with gold, silver, and precious gems. We are encouraged to store this wisdom securely within our hearts, protecting it from the corruptive influences of the world.

Navigating life with this divine wisdom can sometimes feel like a tug of war. We might find ourselves pulled between God's eternal wisdom and our finite understanding. Success in this spiritual struggle requires aligning ourselves with God, ensuring that we are not merely relying on our perceptions of wisdom but are fully embracing His guidance.

Embracing Redemption's Jewels

God is generously scattering redemption jewels from heaven, beckoning us to grasp His wisdom. As He proclaims, "I'm giving you Redemption, my jewels to my people." Malachi 3:17 describes us as His "treasured possession," endowed with beauty, strength, and protection—attributes

COURAGE: A REDEMPTION STORY

often linked with wisdom, grace, and compassion. Through redemption, God not only saves us but adorns us with these divine qualities, making us His shining jewels.

I learned a valuable lesson about God's redemption jewels in finances. My husband and I did not have a budget; we would spend with no accountability. I kept receiving words that I would be wealthy, and even my name, Lacricia, means wealth. I thought my bank account did not look wealthy. One day, Dave Ramsey was offering a free course for veterans, and I decided to take it.

Once I followed his principles of budgeting, saving, and paying off the smallest bill first, our finances began to increase, and our savings started to grow. We began receiving financial blessings as a result. I realized that it was as simple as budgeting. Now, I give an account for every dime we spend, and this has truly been a redemption jewel from heaven over our finances.

God knows what each of us needs to be financially set free. He will never lead us wrongly; we must trust Him. Now, when emergencies arise, we have the finances ready, and we don't have to use a credit card and rack up a lot of interest. God wants us to owe no man anything but love. As it says in Romans 13:8 (NIV), "Let no debt remain outstanding, except the continuing debt to love one another, for whoever loves others has fulfilled the law."

We had always given our tithes, but nothing was working until we began to budget. God wants us to be proactive in doing what He has called us to do, like budgeting, giving to others, and helping His church. This journey has taught me that following God's wisdom in financial matters can lead to true freedom and blessings.

Adorned by God's transformative power, we are likened to refined gemstones, each reflecting His love like jewels in a crown Zechariah 9:16-17. With the assurance of our redeemed identity, God plants us afresh in fertile ground, ensuring that the challenges once hardening our lives soften, allowing us and our families to grow and flourish continuously.

CONTINUOUS GROWTH AND PROTECTION

Just as daisies bloom multiple times and lavenders throughout the year, redemption renews us daily. In every season of life, God's redemptive work is manifest, promising new beginnings and continual growth. This cycle of renewal is beautifully captured in 2 Corinthians 5:17, where God invites us to embrace the new life sprouting from the ashes—life that creates vibrant gardens and fields wrapped in His beauty.

Daisies and Lavenders

Living with God's wisdom has instilled a deep courage within me, enabling me to stand against injustices, particularly within the church. Church leaders must be held accountable for their actions, as their behavior deeply impacts the spiritual well-being of their congregations. Experiencing church hurt first hand has reinforced my commitment to advocate for those who suffer similar pains. This advocacy is rooted in the understanding that manipulation and mistreatment have no place in God's plan for His people.

The journey of wisdom is ongoing and dynamic, involving continuous learning, growth, and the application of God's truth to every aspect of our lives. It equips us to navigate life's complexities with clarity and purpose, ensuring that we live not just for ourselves, but as beacons of God's light and love in the world.

PRACTICAL STEPS FOR EMBRACING WISDOM AND REDEMPTION

To truly embrace wisdom and redemption in your life, here are some practical steps that have helped me along my journey:

- **Seek God's Guidance**: Always pray and ask God for wisdom in every decision. As it says in James 1:5, "If any of you lacks wisdom, you should ask God, who gives generously to all without finding fault, and it will be given to you."
- **Budgeting and Financial Stewardship**: Follow biblical principles for managing your finances. Take courses, read books, and seek advice from trusted financial advisors who align with godly wisdom.
- **Accountability and Mentorship**: Surround yourself with mentors and accountability partners who will support you in your spiritual growth and practical living.

- **Continual Learning**: Stay committed to learning more about God's word and His ways. Attend classes, read scripture, and engage in discussions that deepen your understanding of divine wisdom.
- **Embrace Community**: Engage with a faith community that encourages and uplifts you. Share your struggles and victories, and support others in their journeys as well.
- **Stand Against Injustice**: Be courageous in standing up against wrongs, especially within the church. Advocate for integrity and righteousness in all areas of life.

CONCLUSION

As we continue to grow in God's wisdom and embrace His redemption, we become reflections of His glory, living testimonies of His grace. Our lives, adorned with the jewels of wisdom and redemption, shine brightly for all to see, leading others to the source of true life and eternal hope. Through continuous learning, practical application, and unwavering faith, we can navigate life's complexities and fulfill the divine purposes set before us.

Chapter 9

RECONCILIATION AND REDEMPTION

Michaela and I

2 Corinthians 5:18-19 "All this is from God, who reconciled us to himself through Christ and gave us the ministry of reconciliation: that God was reconciling the world to himself in Christ, not counting people's sins against them. And he has committed to us the message of reconciliation."

When my daughter Michaela was growing up, we had a pretty good relationship. She was a happy child who loved her family and friends. However, once Michaela became a teenager, she started to have different views about herself and God. This was troubling to me. She started saying she believed in God, but not in the Bible. This was the same little girl who would have encounters with angels. I found it disturbing. Then, I found out she was attracted to the same sex. I was devastated and confused. I thought, where did this come from? She would later tell me she had these feelings since she was a child. I would ask her why, when in previous conversations, she would say she was going to marry a man and have children. This new view caused us to bump heads.

In my mind, I thought that a woman should be with a man, not a woman with a woman. This was my view growing up. We never had an issue with same-sex relationships, but I just didn't understand what was happening. This caused her to say I hated her and didn't like her. I said none of those things were true, but I have my beliefs just like she had hers. This caused turmoil in our relationship. One day, she said she was moving in with her girlfriend and that they were going to get married. I asked God what was going on. As a mother, I tried to fix it, wondering if I did something wrong. She said, "Yes, you were never there for me." I was shocked, because we were always together. I thought I was being punished. I couldn't accept it until one Sunday when my pastor taught a series about this, and it opened my eyes to see it in a different light. It was like a revelation—I needed to show unconditional love. But during this time, she just stopped talking to me. I would call, and she wouldn't answer. I would text, and she would give one-word responses. It took two years for her to call home.

Every year, beginning in January, I would do a 21-day fast. I would inquire of the Lord for His directions for me and my family. On January 14th, 2021, I heard the Lord say that she was going to call. She was in a very dark place, but I needed to keep praying for her. I was excited as I waited and waited. The process was up and down, and I began to doubt God because this prophecy took place two years later. I thought, did I really hear God? But then, I would get other words confirming this about prodigals coming home. Two years later, Dwayne and I received a call from her. I was overjoyed with emotion. Once we began to talk, we both started crying, saying how long it had been and how much we missed each other. We promised never to become estranged again. We had a long conversation that day, which started many more conversations in the future. We just picked up where we left off. I went to see her in Texas, and we got to spend Thanksgiving together, hang out, and just love on her. Her siblings really missed her a lot. It was great to see God's reconciliation at work.

I believe this for other parents or families who are waiting to hear from loved ones: just trust God in the process. He is not a man that He should lie or have to repent. God is faithful, and we need to wait. We learned that family is the most important thing in life. Without family, we have nothing but broken relationships. We were able to forgive one another and move forward in our healing process. We learned to let each other share their views without trying to make the other think the way we do.

THE ROLE OF PRAYER

During this challenging period, prayer became my lifeline. I prayed for wisdom, patience, and the ability to show unconditional love. Prayer provided me with the strength to continue reaching out to Michaela, even when it seemed like there was no hope. Through prayer, I learned to trust in God's timing and His ability to heal and restore relationships.

One specific prayer experience stands out. There was a night when I was feeling particularly hopeless and overwhelmed by the distance between Michaela and me. I cried out to God, asking Him to show me a sign that He was working on her heart. The next morning, I received a text from Michaela, a simple "Good morning, Mom." It was the first time she had initiated contact in months. That small message was a huge encouragement and a reminder that God hears our prayers and is always at work, even when we can't see it.

LESSONS LEARNED

- **Trust in God's Timing**: God's plans often unfold differently than we expect. Trusting in His timing is crucial, even when it feels like nothing is happening.

- **Unconditional Love**: Showing unconditional love, even when we disagree with our loved ones, is essential. This love can bridge gaps and heal wounds.
- **Patience and Persistence**: Reconciliation can be a long and challenging process. Patience and persistence in prayer and love are necessary.
- **Open Communication**: Allowing each other to express their views without judgment fosters understanding and healing.
- **Practical Steps for Reconciliation**
- **Commit to Prayer**: Regularly pray for your loved ones, seeking God's guidance and intervention in their lives.
- **Show Unconditional Love**: Make a conscious effort to show love and support, regardless of disagreements or differences.
- **Seek God's Wisdom**: Ask God for wisdom in your interactions and decisions, trusting Him to guide you.
- **Be Patient**: Understand that reconciliation is a process and may take time. Trust in God's timing and remain hopeful.
- **Encourage Open Dialogue**: Foster an environment where open and honest communication is welcomed and respected.

Chapter 10

FINDING WHERE I BELONG

This journey of wisdom has not only deepened my understanding, but has also led me to a profound sense of acceptance and belonging. Learning that I do not need to seek validation through others' acceptance was transformative; my value is inherent because of who I am in Christ. This revelation has liberated me to express my authentic self without fear of judgment or the need to conform to external expectations, allowing me to thrive in environments that affirm my identity and nurture my spiritual growth.

In my past, the absence of a healthy father figure and painful experiences within the church clouded my perception of acceptance. These struggles made it challenging to perceive God as a loving father. Yet, as I navigated my faith journey, I encountered the unwavering and unconditional acceptance of God. Understanding that He loves and accepts us completely transformed my perspective, empowering me to face life with newfound confidence and grace.

Ephesians 1:5 reminds us, "He predestined us for adoption to sonship through Jesus Christ, in accordance with his pleasure and will." This scripture beautifully encapsulates the divine acceptance that each of us can embrace.

Through these experiences, I have come to understand my identity and God's purpose for my life. I am a warrior—strong, resilient, and designed to help others succeed. Embracing that I am more than enough, I learned that there is no need to compare myself to others; we are all uniquely crafted in God's image, each with a distinct path and purpose. This realization that God has a plan for each of us requires that we actively participate and walk alongside Him—it will not just fall into our laps.

Finding where I truly belong has been a journey of stepping into the roles that God designed for me. I am now a teacher, a poet, a writer, and a leader in the arts community. Roles I could never have fully embraced without recognizing who God created me to be. Being a part of our Art Community at Church has been a significant part of my growth, where I contribute and continue to learn.

I am profoundly thankful that I did not give up on myself, for I know that God will never give up on us. Every step of this journey has reinforced the power of divine acceptance and the peace that comes with finding one's place in the world.

One specific experience that stands out is when I was invited to lead a workshop at our church's arts community. Initially, I was nervous and doubted my ability to teach others. However, I prayed for guidance and felt God's reassurance. The workshop was a success, and many participants shared how they felt inspired and uplifted. This experience solidified my understanding of God's purpose for me and boosted my confidence to continue pursuing my passions.

I encourage each of you reading this book to embark on this journey of self-discovery and to seek the acceptance that comes from God alone. It is a path filled with challenges and revelations, but most importantly, it is a journey that leads to a life lived fully and freely in the identity God has given you.

PRACTICAL STEPS FOR FINDING ACCEPTANCE AND BELONGING

- **Seek God's Guidance**: Regularly pray and ask God to reveal His purpose for your life. Jeremiah 29:11 reminds us that God has plans to prosper us and give us hope and a future.
- **Embrace Your Unique Identity**: Recognize that you are uniquely created by God. Celebrate your strengths and embrace your weaknesses, knowing that God can use all aspects of your life for His glory.
- **Join a Community**: Surround yourself with supportive and like-minded individuals who encourage your spiritual growth and affirm your identity in Christ. Engage in church activities, small groups, or any community that aligns with your values.

- **Pursue Your Passions**: Identify and pursue the passions and talents that God has placed in your heart. Whether it's teaching, writing, or any other talent, use it to glorify God and serve others.
- **Reflect on Scripture**: Regularly read and meditate on scriptures that speak to your identity and God's promises. Scriptures like Psalm 139:14 ("I praise you because I am fearfully and wonderfully made; your works are wonderful, I know that full well.") can reinforce your understanding of self-worth.

By following these steps and trusting in God's plan, you can find true acceptance and belonging in the unique identity He has given you.

Part 4:

Father to the Fatherless

Chapter 11

IN HIS LOVING PRESENCE

After receiving God's acceptance, His presence in my life became tangibly real. I began to experience the depth of His love in a way that was entirely new to me, feeling as though I was sitting on His lap, hearing His comforting words directly. For someone who had never felt a father's love, these encounters were profoundly transformative. He filled me with His Spirit, and the spiritual nourishment I received during prayer sessions deepened my connection to Him. He reassured me repeatedly that He is a father to the fatherless and encouraged me to embrace Him as my own.

With each divine encounter, I grew closer to understanding God as a loving father. The feelings of rejection that had haunted me began to dissipate, replaced by a profound sense of acceptance. Fear and insecurity faded as I learned to trust God more fully, finding peace in His unconditional love. I stopped comparing myself to others and embraced the unique individual He created me to be.

Psalm 68:5 says, "A father to the fatherless, a defender of widows, is God in his holy dwelling." This scripture became a cornerstone in my journey, reminding me of God's unwavering presence and love.

This transformation also awakened a new identity within me as a worshiper. My daily worship became a vital expression of my life, deeply personal and heartfelt. Those around me noticed a change; they were moved by the authenticity and intensity of my worship, often moved to tears by the sight of my family and I worshiping together. What I had once dismissed—my ability to lead in prayer—had become central to my life, reflecting the profound changes God was working within me.

One specific experience that stands out is when I was leading our Sunday morning prayer session at church. As I prayed, I felt an overwhelming sense of God's presence, and I could see the congregation being touched by the Spirit. People were lifting their hands, crying, and connecting deeply with God. This experience reinforced my calling and showed me the power of prayer in bringing people closer to God.

Another significant moment was during a treasure hunt in the park, where we would seek God's guidance to find people who needed His love and words of encouragement. I approached a homeless person and shared a word that I felt the Lord had given me. To my amazement, the word was right on point, and the person received it with tears, acknowledging that God was speaking directly to them. Seeing how a simple act of obedience could bring comfort and hope to someone in need filled my heart with joy and strengthened my faith in hearing from the Lord.

I encourage each of you reading this book to embark on this journey of self-discovery and to seek the acceptance that comes from God alone. It is a path filled with challenges and revelations, but most importantly, it is a journey that leads to a life lived fully and freely in the identity God has given you.

PRACTICAL STEPS FOR CULTIVATING GOD'S PRESENCE

- **Daily Prayer**: Spend time in daily prayer, seeking to hear God's voice and feel His presence.
- **Worship**: Incorporate worship into your daily routine, whether through singing, listening to worship music, or reflecting on God's goodness.
- **Scripture Reading**: Regularly read and meditate on scriptures that speak to God's love and fatherhood, such as Psalm 68:5.
- **Community**: Surround yourself with a faith community that supports and encourages your spiritual growth.
- **Journaling**: Keep a journal of your spiritual experiences and encounters with God. Reflecting on these can strengthen your faith and help you see God's hand in your life.

Acts of Kindness: Engage in activities like treasure hunts or outreach missions where you can share God's love and words of encouragement with others in need.

As believers, we are often gifted with dreams and visions directly from God. These are not just fleeting images, but divine calls to action. Embracing them requires an unwavering focus on God—an "Audience of One." Colossians 3:23-24 (NIV) exhorts us to work heartily, as for the Lord rather than for men, reminding us that our ultimate reward comes from Him. In these moments, when we dedicate our actions and dreams to God alone, we enter a profound partnership with Him.

WHAT DOES IT MEAN TO HAVE AN AUDIENCE OF ONE?

Alone with Father God

An audience of one with God means maintaining an intense, uninterrupted focus on Him. It involves shutting out distractions, doubts, and fears, allowing God to lead you through the dreams He has imparted to you. This connection is not fleeting—it requires sustained adoration and attention, where nothing else can draw your gaze away from Him.

This kind of relationship is about more than just acknowledging God's presence; it's about constantly interacting with Him, seeking His guidance step-by-step, and trusting in His timing. Our dreams may be unique, and while it's tempting to look to others or rush ahead, God's personalized path for us is where true fulfillment lies.

I cannot live without God's presence in my life. It is like our heartbeat, constantly beating to His presence and guidance. God is always encountering us, even when we don't see or feel it.

Learning from the Divine Teacher

John 17:3 emphasizes the importance of knowing God intimately: "Now this is eternal life: that they know you, the only true God, and Jesus Christ, whom you have sent." Understanding who God is, fundamentally changes how we pursue our dreams. For instance, when I dreamed of creating a new shampoo bottle, I embarked on a learning journey. Though the path was fraught with frustration, especially when I tried to forge ahead on my own or mimic others' successes, I learned to rely solely on God's guidance.

Trusting in God and understanding His nature are crucial. I maintain a dream journal, documenting how God communicates with me. This record is a tangible reminder of His faithfulness and guidance, helping me to discern His voice clearly and follow His lead without confusion or distraction.

I remember early in my journey after giving my life to God, I attended a women's breakfast. During this event, I distinctly heard the Lord say, "Bow down before me." I was stunned and wondered where this voice was coming from. When I opened my eyes, I saw most of the women bowing down. I was amazed to hear God's voice so early on in my walk. It brought so much joy to my life, knowing that I could hear His voice. It felt like a warm embrace all around me.

PRACTICAL STEPS FOR EMBRACING DIVINE ENCOUNTERS

- **Dream Journal**: Keep a dedicated journal to record dreams and visions. Reflect on them regularly to understand how God communicates with you.
- **Focused Prayer**: Spend time in focused prayer, asking God for clarity and direction regarding the dreams and visions He has given you.
- **Scripture Study**: Immerse yourself in scriptures that reinforce God's promises and His guidance. Colossians 3:23-24 and John 17:3 are excellent starting points.
- **Seek Godly Counsel**: Surround yourself with spiritually mature individuals who can provide wise counsel and encouragement as you pursue your divine dreams.
- **Patience and Trust**: Practice patience and trust in God's timing. Understand that His path for you may not be immediate, but it will always be the best.

By following these steps, you can deepen your relationship with God and clearly understand the dreams and visions He has placed within you.

Chapter 11

IN HIS LOVING PRESENCE

As stated in Luke 21:25-28, we are reminded of the signs of the times and the assurance of redemption drawing near. This scripture reinforces the promise of God's ultimate redemption, not just in the eschatological sense, but in every aspect of our lives. God's plan is to redeem us, to restore relationships, and to bring His people back to Him.

In every challenge, whether personal or global, the invitation is to lift our heads and look forward because our redemption is near. This redemption is not only about eternal salvation, but also about the here and now—God redeeming our daily struggles, healing our broken relationships, and using our trials for His glory.

Embracing this promise means maintaining a posture of forgiveness, continually trusting in God's ability to redeem and heal. It involves having a support system, but most importantly, it requires an unwavering faith in God's plan and timing. No matter what we face, we are assured that God is with us, guiding and directing our steps toward His perfect will.

By embracing His wisdom, celebrating His presence, and relying on His strength, we can live lives marked by divine acceptance, deep gratitude, and the courage to face whatever comes with a steadfast and hopeful heart.

LIVING WATERS: THE SPIRITUAL IRRIGATION SYSTEM

Irrigation System of the Lord

Just as irrigation is essential for the vitality of crops, spiritual irrigation nourishes our souls. In agriculture, irrigation involves the artificial application of water to soil, often enriched with nutrients to foster plant growth. Similarly, our spiritual lives thrive when nurtured by the Holy Spirit, which waters us with grace and wisdom.

Paul enlightens us in 1 Corinthians 12:13, explaining that all believers have been given the Holy Spirit to drink. The original Greek term for "given a drink" translates to "irrigate," illustrating our need to be saturated with divine presence. This spiritual saturation is crucial for our growth and health, just as water is vital for plants.

Our souls, much like soil, require regular spiritual watering. Isaiah 44:3-4 promises that God will pour water on the thirsty and streams on the dry ground, an allegory for blessing His people with spiritual vitality. Without this constant nourishment from the Holy Spirit, our spiritual lives can become dry and stagnant, unable to bear fruit.

MAINTAINING THE FLOW

To keep the spiritual waters flowing, engage in practices that foster a deep and continual connection with the Holy Spirit. Regular prayer, meditation on Scripture, participation in community worship, and the pursuit of spiritual disciplines help maintain this essential connection.

BENEFITS

Regularly irrigated by the Holy Spirit, individuals experience growth in virtues such as peace, joy, and resilience. Collectively, when a community is spiritually nourished, it becomes robust and flourishing, capable of overcoming challenges and supporting its members in times of need.

OVERCOMING SPIRITUAL DROUGHTS

At times, everyone experiences spiritual droughts. During these phases, it's crucial to seek the Holy Spirit actively and ask for renewal. Strategies such as intensifying prayer life, seeking fellowship with other believers, and participating in spiritual retreats can help restore vitality.

Imagine your life as a garden that, under the care of the Divine Gardener, is thriving and blooming. The Holy Spirit's irrigation ensures that despite the occasional dry spells, your spiritual garden remains vibrant and fruitful.

Apple Tree

THE APPLE OF HIS EYES POEM

I am loved by Him, I thought it was grim to be His beloved.

I am the apple of His eyes, no more lies.

I have tasted and seen His goodness and mercy

Under His shade of protection for me.

I see His delight in me,

I feel safe in His presence under the shadow of His wings.

He has shown me His grace and mercy, no more being thirsty.

My desires have been satisfied.

I will forever rest in my beloved's presence,

Covered by His unfailing love.

As I delved into the study of apple trees and their robust root systems, I discovered how these roots, known for their strength and depth, provide a stable foundation that supports the tree's growth and fruit production. Similarly, in our spiritual journeys, these roots can symbolize the deep, enduring foundations of faith and resilience that sustain us, especially after we've experienced transformation through God's grace.

Just as apple tree roots draw nutrients from the soil to nourish the tree, a person rooted in God's Word and love draws spiritual nourishment that fosters growth and maturity. God desires for us to be deeply rooted in the truths of His redemption, nourished by His divine love and wisdom, enabling us to flourish in all aspects of life, including our spiritual, emotional, and relational growth.

Moreover, the roots beneath an apple tree not only support the tree itself but can also connect with the roots of other trees, forming an interconnected system. This illustrates how God encourages us to be a community in redemption, sharing our experiences and supporting one another. He does not intend for us to be isolated; we need each other just as the apple tree relies on its roots for support.

Song of Songs 2:3 beautifully captures this imagery: "Like an apple tree among the trees of the forest, is my beloved among the young men. I am delighted to sit in his shade, and his fruit is sweet to my taste."

This verse reminds us that God seeks to be our shade and our covering, delighting us when we rest in His presence. Similarly, Colossians 2:7

teaches us to be "rooted and built up in Him, strengthened in the faith as you were taught, and overflowing with thankfulness." This grounding is essential for enduring the process of redemption. God does not want us to remain barren; He desires for us to be fruitful in every aspect of life.

Consider the story of Hannah, who faced barrenness and endured ridicule and immense anguish. Imagine her distress at seeing others with children while she remained unable to conceive. Yet, her fervent prayers in the temple, where she was mistaken for being inebriated due to her intense mourning, exemplify her deep yearning and the strength of her spiritual roots.

I, too, recall a time when I felt similarly barren, mourning deeply after my mother's passing. The pain was so profound that I would cry daily, pleading with God to alleviate my suffering. It seemed endless, but I continued to pour my heart out before the Lord until one day, I realized the pain had subsided. I am profoundly grateful for God's presence during those times of deep sorrow, just as He was there for Hannah, answering her prayers with the gift of a son.

In our moments of deepest need, when we feel barren and desolate, our spiritual roots—strengthened by faith, nourished by God's word, and supported by our community—can sustain and eventually lead us to a place of fruitfulness and joy.

Lily among Thorns

I AM HIS LILY POEM

I am His Lily among the Thorns Born in His field.

I had to yield to His delight as His precious darling.

No more quarreling within.

I begin to see His eyes, no more lies.

I have felt His affection for me.

I feel safe in His arms.

I have His charm as a woman,

No more being thirsty.

My desires are now quenched, I will forever bloom as His beautiful young beloved,

Flourishing in His eternal embrace.

The natural world mirrors this redemptive cycle in profound ways. Consider how a barren field, when nourished and cared for, transforms into a fertile landscape teeming with life. Similarly, our lives, once marred by barrenness and despair, can flourish under God's redemptive care. Just like an apple tree that once stood dormant, but later bursts into a display of blossoms and fruit, our lives too can reflect such fruitfulness.

Drawing from firsthand experiences, this concept becomes even more poignant. Reflect on moments of personal barrenness—emotional, spiritual, or relational—that seemed insurmountable. Yet, through faith and the transformative power of God's redemption, what was once barren can become abundantly fruitful. This personal transformation not only impacts our own lives, but also influences those around us, highlighting God's power to bring redemption to the most desolate of circumstances.

As we grow and change, God's protection is a constant presence. It shields us from reverting to our old ways and supports us as we explore new facets of our redeemed selves. This protection is crucial, as it guards not just our spiritual well-being but also our emotional and physical realms, ensuring that the growth we experience is healthy and sustainable.

Embrace the journey of continuous redemption with open arms and a willing heart. Recognize that each phase of growth brings its challenges and triumphs, but under God's nurturing care, every season is an opportunity for deeper transformation and greater fruitfulness. As we move forward, let us hold onto the promise that our redemptive journey is not only about overcoming the past, but also about embracing an ever-renewing future filled with potential and hope.

Praise/Thanksgiving

1 Thessalonians 5:16-18 (NIV): "Rejoice always, pray continually, give thanks in all circumstances; for this is God's will for you in Christ Jesus."

I am profoundly thankful for God's forgiveness, which has reshaped my entire existence. I recognize that I am not perfect, but I am being perfected by His hand. His guidance and direction are steadfast, even when I stray. His corrections are always gentle, designed to realign me with His divine purposes. He has promised never to let us give up on ourselves, because He has created each of us for a special purpose.

I am grateful for the family God has given me—my grandchildren, my husband, my friends, and my church family. Each of these relationships has been a channel of God's love and a mirror reflecting His grace in my life. I wouldn't trade my walk with God for anything the world could offer, for in Him I find true fulfillment and purpose.

As we close this journey together, I invite you to also find your voice of praise and thanksgiving. Let us not take for granted the daily renewals and the small victories along our paths. May we always recognize the beauty in the transformation that God orchestrates in our lives and respond with heartfelt gratitude and joy. In praise, we find strength, and in thanksgiving, we recognize the vastness of God's blessings.

My mountain Top

THANKFUL POEM

I am thankful.

I started up the mountain,

with His vision in my mind. I am sound. I

feel His presence all around, leading me to victory.

I am a warrior princess standing tall. With my sword in my hands

I will never fall. Now I stand bold and courageous,

In my redemption. I am glamorous,

to tell that you too shall rise above it all.

ACKNOWLEDGMENTS

First and foremost, I want to thank God. Without Him, this would not be possible. I am humbled and grateful that He chose me to share my story. His grace and guidance have been the foundation of this journey.

I would like to dedicate a special tribute to my beloved mother Dee who passed away in 2009. She was a strong and courageous woman who taught me invaluable lessons that continue to guide me today. Her unwavering strength and determination held our family together through all of life's challenges. Mom, your love and wisdom have been my constant inspiration, and this book is a testament to the values and resilience you instilled in me to stay strong and never give up no matter what storms arise. I miss you every day and am forever grateful for the legacy you left behind.

To my children and grandchildren, your love and support have been my anchor. To my husband, Dwayne, thank you for standing by my side. To my children—Portia, Timothy, Michaela, and Uzziah—you are my pride and joy. To my grandchildren— Aniyah-Marie, Jordin, and Alanni—you bring light and laughter into my life.

I am deeply grateful to my sisters, Amintha and Geraldine my brother-in-law Nathaniel and to my brothers, Chris and Robert. My sisters Patricia and Anndolyn, who has since passed away, is forever in my heart. To my nieces, nephews and cousins on both sides thank you for your encouragement and the joy you bring into our family. A special thanks to my mother-in-law, Rosa.

To my friends, my Create Academy family, and all those who prayed for me and spoke words of encouragement, I am so thankful. Margie, thank you for encouraging me to teach "Create to Be Free," for allowing me partner with you and Katy in the arts community at BridgeWay Church, and for being by my side every step of the way. For Iris who introduced me to Bridgeway and create to be free and for everyone's support during my ups and downs, your willingness to listen to my cries, heartache and share in my joys, has meant the world to me. A special thank you to Theresa for being a leader and mentor who believed in me and my gifts. To all my mentors Charlotte, Bette, and Flora who left an invaluable mark on my spiritual life.

To my church family at BridgeWay Church, thank you for your prophetic words and continual encouragement. Papa(Apostle) Peter and Mama Gwen, your words of truth is a testament that following God will always lead to victory. To Amy from Colorado Prays and Justin, who I pray with weekly, your partnership in prayer has been a blessing. And to Teia, Mary Ann , Petra, Kat and the many others who walked me through inner healing, and deliverance I am deeply thankful for your guidance and support.

Thank you all who took my calling seriously, and who did not judge me or talk about me, but prayed earnestly for me, my calling, family, health, my marriage, both past and present. For the thousands of prayers you've lifted up for me— without them, where would I be?

Lastly, to everyone who has played a part in my life, whether mentioned here or not, know that you have left an indelible mark on my heart. I am forever grateful for each and every one of you.

Her upcoming book, *Forged in the Fire: The Spiritual Path of the Sword*, promises to take readers on another transformative journey, exploring the deeper spiritual meanings behind one of history's most powerful symbols.

AUTHOR'S NOTE

As I embarked on the journey of writing *Courage: A Redemption Story*, I was guided by the belief that our stories—no matter how painful—hold the power to heal not only ourselves but others who may walk similar paths. This book is a testament to the transformative power of forgiveness, redemption and courage.

Thank you for reading Courage: A Redemption Story. I hope this book has inspired you on your journey of healing, forgiveness, and redemption. If you found this book helpful, I invite you to explore more resources and join a community dedicated to creative expression and spiritual growth.

Visit https://learn.theresadedmon.com to connect with others on a similar journey, access valuable tools, and become part of a supportive community led by Theresa Dedmon.

Please consider sharing this book with others who might benefit from its message. Your review on Apple Books and my website www.courageandredemption.com would be greatly appreciated and helps spread the word.